RAGDOLLS

MARYSA STORM

Black Rabbit Books

Bolt Jr. is published by Black Rabbit Books
P.O. Box 227, Mankato, Minnesota, 56002.
www.blackrabbitbooks.com
Copyright © 2025 Black Rabbit Books

Alissa Thielges, editor
Rhea Magaro, designer

All rights reserved. No part of this book may be reproduced in any form without written permission from the publisher.

Names: Storm, Marysa, author.
Title: Ragdolls / by Marysa Storm.
Description: Mankato, MN: Black Rabbit Books, [2025] | Series: Bolt Jr. Our favorite cats | Includes bibliographical references and index. | Audience: Ages 5-8 | Audience: Grades K-1
Identifiers: LCCN 2024010403 (print) | LCCN 2024010404 (ebook) | ISBN 9781644666791 (library binding) | ISBN 9781644666975 (ebook)
Subjects: LCSH: Ragdoll cat—Juvenile literature.
Classification: LCC SF449.R34 S767 2025 (print) | LCC SF449.R34 (ebook) | DDC 636.8/3—dc23/eng/20240425
LC record available at https://lccn.loc.gov/2024010403
LC ebook record available at https://lccn.loc.gov/2024010404

Image Credits

Getty Images/bojanstory, 1; Shutterstock/Eric Isselee, 10, Erik Lam, 8–9, 21, Esin Deniz, 5, Iryna Zaichenko Dneprstok, 15, Nils Jacobi, 12, Nynke van Holten, 4, Polina Tomtosova, 3, 24, Pony3000, 19, Ria Peene, 18, Serita Vossen, 23, Snowice_81, 17, Tatyana Vyc, 11, 20–21, Timolina, cover, Tom Wang, 7, Valerio Pardi, 6, Zharinova Marina, 13

Contents

Chapter 1
Meet the Ragdoll..... 4

Chapter 2
Personality............ 10

Chapter 3
Ragdoll Care.......... 16

More Information......... 22

CHAPTER 1

Meet the Ragdoll

Look at that big, fluffy cat. A girl pets it. The cat purrs loudly. It is very relaxed. In fact, it is so relaxed, it goes **limp**! The girl laughs. She is happy her cat is so **content**.

limb: soft and loose

content: feeling pleased and happy

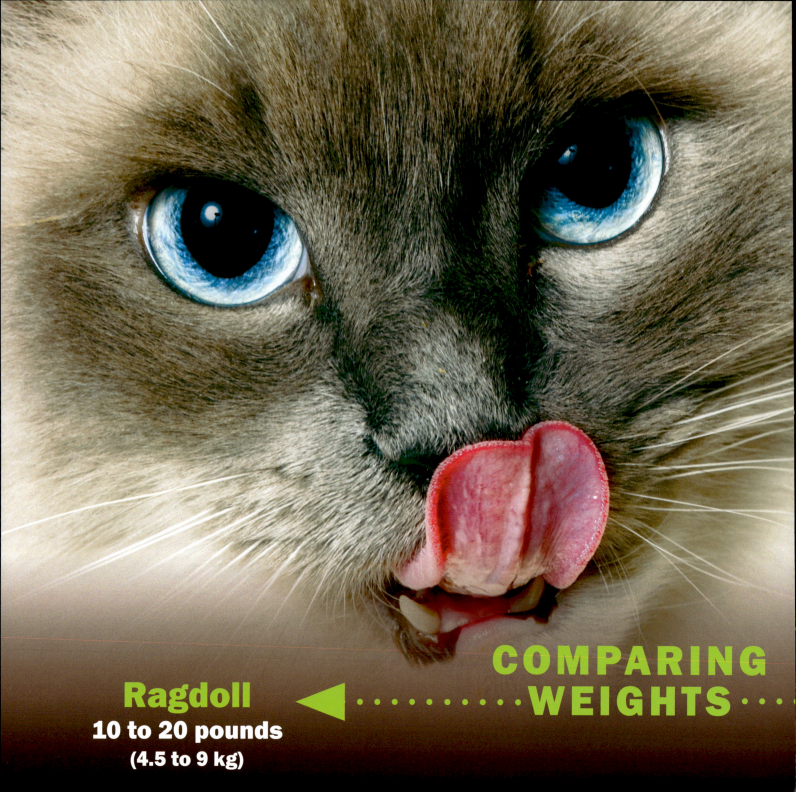

COMPARING WEIGHTS

Ragdoll
10 to 20 pounds
(4.5 to 9 kg)

Big and Fluffy

Ragdolls are big cats. They have giant blue eyes. Their coats are long. They are often gray, cream, red, or brown. The cats have a pointed coat. That means their face, ears, feet, and tail are darker in color.

American Shorthair
6 to 15 pounds
(3 to 7 kg)

PARTS OF A Ragdoll

long coat

long tail

CHAPTER 2

Personality

These cats are gentle and relaxed. They follow their owners around. They love to lay in their owner's lap for nap time. Many people think the cats act like dogs. They say ragdoll cats are very **loyal**.

loyal: being faithful to someone

10

FACT

Some ragdolls play fetch.

11

Playful Cats

Ragdoll cats are playful and sweet. They enjoy games. But owners should be careful when playing with them. It is easy to be too **rough** with these floppy cats.

rough: in a hard or hurtful way

Where They Come From

California

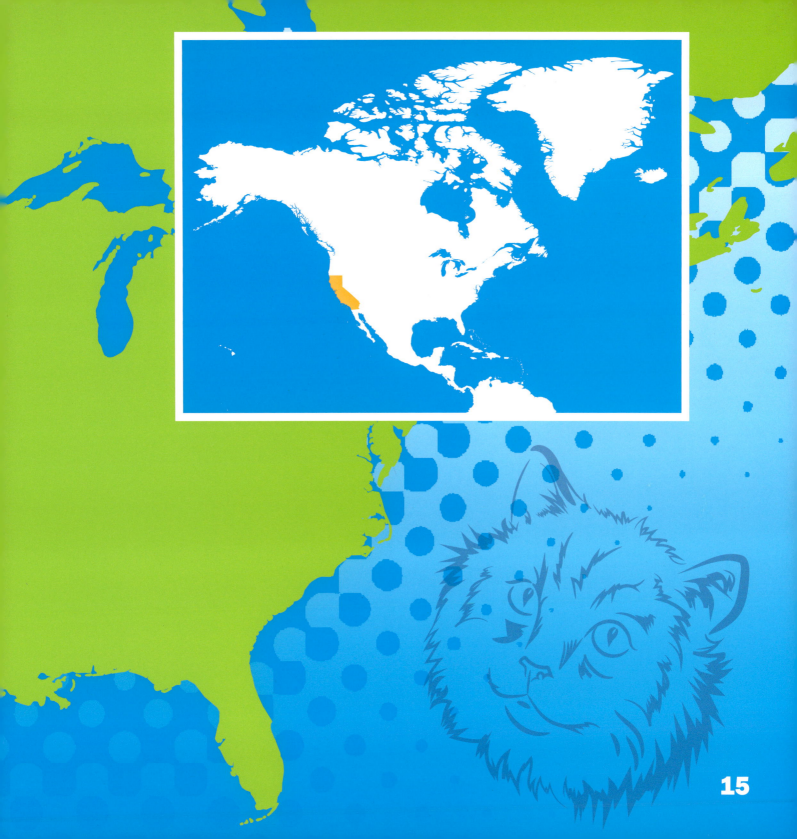

CHAPTER 3

Ragdoll Care

These cats need food and water every day. They also need help grooming. Their long coats should be brushed twice a week. Without brushing, their coat will get tangled.

FACT

Ragdolls shed in the spring and summer.

Friendly Felines

Ragdolls need help staying active. They need more brushing than shorthair cats. But owners love their ragdoll cats. These furry friends are worth the work.

Ragdoll Length
up to 40 inches
(up to 102 centimeters)

Bonus Facts

Ragdolls are known for their loud purr.

They are completely white at birth.

They can live to be 17 years old.

20

They are one of the largest **breeds** of housecat.

breeds: a particular type of cat, dog, horse, or other animal

21

READ MORE/WEBSITES

Andrews, Elizabeth. *Ragdoll Cats.* Minneapolis: Cody Koala, an imprint of Pop!, 2023.

Burling, Alexis. *Cats.* Minneapolis: Abdo Publishing Company, 2024.

Wilson, Sierra. *Ragdoll.* New York: Lightbox Learning Inc., 2023.

Ragdoll
kids.britannica.com/students/article/ragdoll/313127

Ragdoll Cat Breed
www.cats.com/cat-breeds/ragdoll

Ragdoll Facts for Kids
kids.kiddle.co/Ragdoll

GLOSSARY

breed (BREED)—a particular type of cat, dog, horse, or other animal

content (kuhn-TENT)—feeling pleased and happy

limp (LIMP)—soft and loose

loyal (LOY-uhl)—being faithful to someone

rough (RUHF)—in a hard or hurtful way

INDEX

B

body parts, 7, 8-9

C

care, 16, 19
colors, 7, 20

L

life span, 20

P

personality, 10, 13
playing, 11, 13

S

size, 6, 7, 19, 21
sound, 4, 20